THE FISHERMAN'S SON

The Spirit of Ramón Navarro

patagonia®

Punta de Lobos. Photo: Joe Curren

At Patagonia, we publish a collection of books that reflect our pursuits and our values—books on wilderness, outdoor sports, innovation, and a commitment to environmental activism.

Copyright 2015 Patagonia Works

Text © Chris Malloy, Matías López, Yasha Hetzel, Dusty Middleton, Kohl Christensen, Josh Berry, Will Carless, Gerry Lopez, Nick Mucha, and Ramón Navarro

Drawings © Russell Crotty

All photograph copyrights are held by the photographers as indicated in captions.

Editor: John Dutton
Photo Editor: Jenning Steger & Sus Corez
Design: Scott Massey & Chris Malloy
Drawings: Russell Crotty
Production: Scott Webber & Rafael Dunn

Printed in China on 100% recycled paper

Cover band, back cover, and this page photos: Jeff Johnson

Library of Congress Control Number 2015930582
Softcover ISBN 978-1-938340-42-0

1%
FOR THE
PLANET.
MEMBER

NEXT SPREAD Ramón Navarro, Punta de Lobos, Chile. Photo: Rodrigo Farias Moreno

Table of Contents

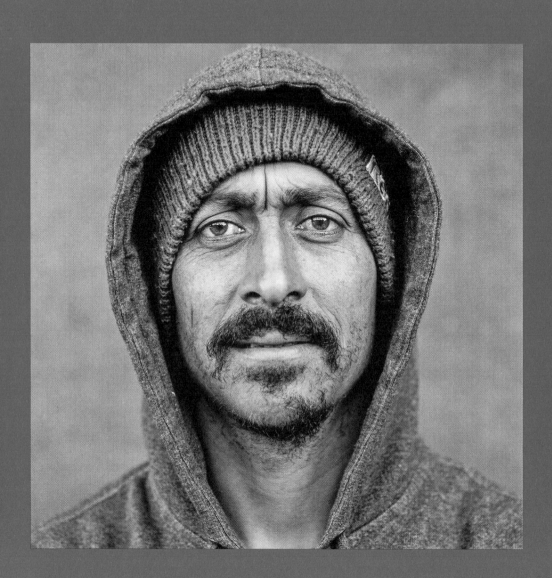

Ramón Alejandro Navarro Rojas.
Photo: Jeff Johnson

INTRO—DUCTION

by Chris Malloy

I ask the old man how long people have been fishing here. He says nothing and instead pulls a small threadbare linen parcel from a wooden box and carefully unwraps it. His face and hands are wind worn, but his gunmetal eyes are lucid and alive.

I'm sitting across the table from four fishermen who have lived their whole lives here at Punta de Lobos. We're in their fish camp. I ask the old man if we can document them harvesting during the next low tide. The old man continues opening the linen and, without looking up, he asks, "What does the ocean mean to you?"

In that moment I realize that I'm not the observer anymore. A thousand things go through my mind, but I settle on "todo"—everything. There is a long silence.

One of the men brings out a boiling pot of fish soup. The sun through the window lights up the steam and it billows through the room. The old man finally looks up and agrees to let my film crew come along, but offers that it might be more useful to bring a net than a camera.

He lays the linen on the table and gently sets the contents down on it. It's a masterfully knapped, deep-green chert arrowhead, a Mapuche artifact used to hunt and fish here thousands of years ago. He takes his soup and leaves me to digest the provenance of the ancient hand-hewn tool that sits before me.

The arrowhead tells the story of the first people to impact this region thousands of years ago. It tells volumes about the Spanish voyagers who landed here in the sixteenth century. It tells something about the nine generations of mixed bloodlines that fished, foraged, and farmed here. Most of all, it tells why Ramón Alejandro Navarro Rojas has a fire in his heart, the will to steward this coastline, and the drive to hunt down the biggest surf on the planet.

He was born here on Punta de Lobos proper and bred of subsistence fishers and foragers. Ramón was raised to provide for his family through a deep understanding of the ocean. He has done that, however, in a way that his forefathers could never have imagined.

He's been described as "coming from nothing to take the big-wave world by storm"—after all he grew up in a subsistence fishing family and became a national hero. But Ramón sees things differently; he believes he was given everything growing up and his accomplishments in giant surf are merely part of a much bigger vision he has for the Chilean coastline.

I've known Ramón for a decade, and I've witnessed much of his uncommon trajectory firsthand. Over the last ten years he has continually set new bars for what humans can accomplish in heavy water. What inspired me to make a film about Ramón, however, is what he's done with the newfound voice his surfing has allowed him in coastal Chile and beyond. The colorful characters that make up the world's big-wave pantheon vary greatly in their path to the top and their motives for what they do. As the following stories and photos show, Ramón's life and motives are completely unique in this realm.

Later that evening, we sit by a wood-burning stove in the home that he built for his family. Ramón holds the Mapuche arrowhead in his hand and looks out to Punta de Lobos. Rising swell readings show that a huge low has descended upon the South Pacific, which means he might be on a plane within forty-eight hours. Another fifty-foot ride would mean more time on the national stage, and another opportunity to speak publicly against the latest development plan proposed just up the coast.

I ask him if he's going to go. Ramón smiles, and as he heads to bed, he says, "Of course, amigo; we are just getting started."

The bounty of the sea and land provides.
Photos: Rodrigo Farias Moreno

01 A Sense of
Place

Chile's central coast. Photo: Dylan Lucas Gordon

In the 1970s, Ramón's parents lived hand-to-mouth on the point overlooking the Morros and his father's favorite fishing hole. When Ramón was born they moved into a house down the beach near Pichilemu. Ramón is sitting on the place of his birth. Punta de Lobos, Chile. Top photo: Jeff Johnson, Bottom photo: Rodrigo Farias Moreno

Ramón knows what he values in life, and it's a way of life, not a bank account balance or something that has to do with material belongings. I think people who spend a lot of time in the ocean and in the wilderness realize that that's where the real value is. I think it's been very helpful for Ramón to be able to travel around the world and to see that it is not going so well everywhere else. And then to realize how rural Chile is in a lot of places, and how many pristine environments there are that are about to be exploited. It's great that somebody like him who has come from humble beginnings has been able to travel around the world and get a better perspective than most of the politicians in Chile. He's in a unique position actually to do a lot of good. — Mark Healey

PAGES 16-18, 20-29, 31-33 On location for the film. Photos: Jeff Johnson

THE EARLY YEARS

by Matías López

In March 1989, another wild summer ended and most surfers returned to their hometowns—most lived in the capital, Santiago. Pichilemu was already the epicenter of central Chile's surfing, but surfing was happening only in summers and on weekends for nearly everybody. When summer ended, the resort town turned back into the fishing village and ghost town it was for the remaining nine months when the hotels, restaurants, and most businesses—and even the beaches—were officially closed.

Just out of high school in Santiago, I had decided to stay and surf, and do whatever it took to survive. I wasn't going back to my hometown of Santiago, wasn't going to college, I wanted to become a fisherman and a real surfer. To understand the ocean, charge big waves, live in front of a classic surf spot. Travel. Explore. Do as the locals did.

After a couple months of wandering, I found myself sharing a funny-looking house with my friend Mando, right in front of Infiernillo, the sometimes-best wave in town. A cool lady had a little shop in a back street where she offered candy, bread, and not much more. I asked if she could wash my clothes, and started frequenting her house. Maria's husband, Jano, was a fisherman, hunter, and storyteller like most of the locals, but he was one of the best. We became good friends, and he generously guided me on how to fish the local waters, and often shared some of his catch.

Jano's oldest kid, Ramón, was probably hiding behind a curtain the first few times I visited; he never appeared. I started noticing him sometime later on the beach, checking the surfing from the rocks.

One day he came up to me after a session at Infiernillo and said, "You did a good turn on that wave." He must have been only ten years old. It was the first time I heard a kid that age comment on surfing in a technical way. Usually people would just ask if you were scared, or if the water was cold. It was clear right away, this kid already understood even before he started surfing.

There had been many local surfers before, and a few were good surfers and competitors, but I had never seen a kid so clear and focused on his goal of becoming a good surfer, the best, a professional.

At first we used to make fun of him for bringing the journalists to his house and telling them of his fisherman's roots: he got more coverage than anybody. Then he got really good, and we didn't make fun of him anymore. Against all the counseling of very worried loved ones, he committed, did everything he had to do, and became Chile's first professional surfer.

Being a natural in the ocean, Ramón quickly evolved into a solid big-wave surfer and barrel maniac. From the kid watching on the rocks, to surfing partner, and eventually to master.

In the years of our beloved *Marejada* surf magazine, he kept pushing the limits and establishing himself as a leader in the professional movement, and especially a leader in the new era of big-wave exploration. I remember two episodes in the early 2000s when I realized that he was stepping onto another level.

We were checking the surf at Infiernillo one day—it looked like eight meters with a side-offshore breeze, top-to-bottom barrels, a set every two minutes, and the lulls had nonstop, three-meter waves. I was happy to just enjoy the show and drink maté, comfortable in my acceptance that the conditions were out of reach. But Ramón was jumping out of his skin; he couldn't take it, he needed a jet ski right away. I just needed another maté. Ramón got himself a jet ski pretty soon and never looked back.

The next time I noticed him take it to another level was at Arica. We had been surfing El Gringo many times and he had already established himself as a standout. He loved cameras, and we ran into this US east coast

Photo: Rodrigo Farias Moreno

crew shooting for *Transworld* magazine. It was big and gnarly, closing out on most of the lefts.

Ramón was going crazy on the close-out bombs, one after another. I feared he would get washed into the rocks, but for some reason he kept coming back out clean. I told him to relax, there was no need to kill himself just because there was a camera in front of him, but he calmly explained how he was in absolute control of his surroundings. He always went for the last wave of the set, having mastered his escape act. He said he was actually letting the few perfect ones that came through go, because he knew there was another one behind.

I truly believe you must seek transcendence in whatever you choose to engage in, and that's what Ramón has done. He has made his own world much larger, and those around him have benefited. He has become a powerful leader of our community, and in these tough times of savage coastal development he has assumed responsibility for taking care of Chile's natural wonders, surf culture, and the unity of our tribe. The task is not easy, and this is just its starting point. From Álvaro Abarca and the pioneers; to my generation; to Ramón, Merello, and Medina; to the kids of today and tomorrow—our heritage is our power and our inspiration.

PREVIOUS SPREAD Four generations of Navarros
in Punta de Lobos LEFT Photo: Rodrigo Farias
Moreno ABOVE The next generation will be facing
major coastal development.

I wish we would have fought a lot harder when I was young, and I wish the guys before me would have fought a lot harder to keep the country country. I see those stickers everywhere on the North Shore and I laugh because most of the people that are running all these stickers are all the rich white people that already bought houses and own everything. They don't want us parking in front of their houses and don't want surf events here because now they've got a little piece of the pie. And the sad part is that Hawaiians are so aggressive now. Hawaiians were so giving back in the day that they gave everything away. It's good to see somebody like Ramón fighting for his people because Chile is like Hawai'i was 200 years ago. Let's keep it that way. Let's keep it for the local people. — Sunny Garcia

RIGHT As developers turn a pristine left pointbreak into a major luxury development, displacing its locals and cutting off beach access, Ramón confronts the gate guard. Puertecillo, central Chile.

NEXT SPREAD Ramón, pictured front and center, hands out relief supplies to people in need after the 8.8 magnitude earthquake in 2010. Photo: Philip Muller

Photo: Rodrigo Farias Moreno

Photo: Scott Aichner

A KNOWL— EDGE OF THE OCEAN

by Yasha Hetzel

In July of 2004 local surfer and hostel owner Kurt Hertrampf organized a big-wave contest in the city of Arica on Chile's parched northern border. Just days into the waiting period, the biggest and cleanest south swell in years appeared in the forecast. Since most of South America's big-wave addicts were already holed up in Kurt's place for the winter, logistics were easy. A media release was mailed out to the local paper, Kurt's Mitsubishi van was parked on a spit of land in front of Playa El Laucho, and scaffolding was set up for the judges.

The waves arrived as forecast, a solid Hawaiian fifteen feet focusing on a Sunset-style peak half a mile offshore under a dusty overcast sky. The hazy conditions were terrible for taking photos, but I set up my camera on a tripod and began clicking away. They were the biggest waves I'd ever seen and the bravery of the local chargers impressed me. Most of the articles I'd seen on Chile had featured professional gringo surfers, scoring "empty" waves. There was usually little, if any, mention of local surfers. The surfing I witnessed that day made me wonder, why not?

The surfers were mostly catching rights off the peak that broke violently but ended in a deep channel after a short ride. The left offered the chance of a much longer ride, but without the safe channel it meant a long treacherous paddle back to the peak. About halfway through the quarterfinals, someone sitting in Kurt's van began madly beeping the horn as a massive set loomed. A distant hooded figure scrambled up the face on the wrong side of the peak and spun around at the last second to freefall down a quadruple overhead wave. At the bottom he reconnected, compressed into a bottom turn, and pulled up into a hollow section half as long as a football field. One, two, three … six seconds passed before the wave spit and Ramón's board fluttered out of the tube, riderless, to the sound of hooting and clapping on the beach.

Ramón didn't make the wave or win the contest, but the photo of the bottom turn eventually ran two pages in the *Surfer's Journal*. It was the first time a major surf magazine outside of Latin America had taken notice of Ramón. At the time, I thought his name would soon be forgotten; the bitter reality is that marketing dollars are usually spent closer to home, and there are more hot surfers around than sponsorship contracts.

Later that year, when the sun came out and sand filled back into the southern point breaks I went to stay with Ramón and his parents in Pichilemu and got a glimpse into the reality of a subsistence fisherman's daily life. I learned how to fillet fish and make empanadas, while uncrowded waves peeled down a sand bottom point down the road.

———

A cloud of white flour hung in the air and dusted Ramón's eyebrows while his fingers worked quickly—twisting, folding, and flattening a lump of dough on the countertop in a back room of the house. He had been baking empanadas as long as he could remember and intuition told him when to add more flour or a splash of water, and when to stop working it and leave it to rise.

In the patio out back, his dad Alejandro, or 'Jano' for short, tended to a crackling fire in a mud brick oven, readying it for the hundred or so seafood pastries we had to make before we could go surfing. It was the Fiestas Patrias holiday weekend and they were planning for extra customers in the family shop out front. Ramón and his father had already spent the early hours of the morning diving in the ocean to gather the ingredients.

As Ramón rolled out the dough and cut the circles that would be folded over a savory mix of fish, onions, and *mariscos*, he told me of his

Photo: Jeff Johnson

upbringing and of his dreams of sponsorship dollars and chasing swells to Mavericks and Hawai'i.

Ramón's pride for his old man and his old man's pride for his son were evident, but they didn't speak much of it. Their relationship was like two mates, joking and making fun of each other; if you told your kid he was the best his ego would swell too big. Better to be humble, work hard, let your actions do the talking.

Dad had taught Ramón that the ocean can give you everything if you know where, when, and how. Jano knew how to take from and give back to the sea. How to keep only what you need, to leave the small fish to grow to become big fish. Ramón listened to his father, but he heeded his father's advice on his own terms. "I can do this with waves," Ramón decided. He loved fishing, but he saw the tough life his family had and thought he saw a way to a brighter future.

"Enough about surfing! Hurry up with those empanadas before the fire goes out!" Jano poked his head in the door, smiled, and winked at me before adding, "And you, gringo, put that camera down and get to work!"

Ramón's argument for a career path as a professional surfer was passionate but to me seemed so far from reality. Ramón's father seemed to agree.

"Appreciate what you have, Ramón," his father told him time after time.

When Ramón finished with the dough, he cut out small circles and spooned in the filling, adding an olive and half a hardboiled egg to each before folding over the dough and crimping down the edges. He carried a wooden tray out to his dad where rolls of *cochayuyo* seaweed and chiles dried under a smoky roof. As they worked side-by-side baking the empanadas in the mud oven, pointing out each other's mistakes, I saw two versions of the same man. One of them middle-aged and balding, with callused hands and a lifetime of lessons learned; the other with a head full of hair, young, eager, and maybe a little bit naïve.

Occasionally as they pulled the steaming empanadas from the oven one would crumble and break and an olive would roll out onto the floor. We took a rest sitting and eating the damaged ones. Ramón's dad looked out into the yard and noticed that the willow tree had stopped swaying in the wind. "You had better get down to Lobos if you want to show this gringo some waves," he said. Ramón jumped up and grabbed his dry smoky wetsuit hanging from the rafters.

"Vamos," he told me. "Let's go!" Twenty minutes later we were in the water, sharing glassy walls with a few friends as the sun set.

———

Now a decade after that sunset, Ramón has achieved his impossible dream. He has a house and money to share with his wife and child, and freedom to travel the world. But he's happiest here at home.

"It took me a long time to realize it," he tells me. " But my dad was right—I have everything here."

These days Ramón is a busy man, but he still finds the time to help out his parents and make empanadas. To this day he says that wave I photographed in Arica was one of the best tubes he's ever had. He dreams of catching it again, putting his experience to use so he can make it out of the tube next time.

He'll teach his son the same lessons as his father taught him. Be humble, dream big. Take care of the ocean, and it will take care of you.

BELOW Ramón's grandmother tells him stories from the early days living in a cave in Punta de Lobos. Photos: Jeff Johnson

Arica, Chile. Photo: Scott Aichner

PREVIOUS SPREAD El Buey, in Arica, like other surf breaks in Chile, faced
threats from development. However, Ramón and the surf community
voiced their opposition to harmful construction and helped preserve
this break. NEXT SPREAD The family storefront where Ramón's family sells
homemade empanadas. PAGES 42-47 Photos: Yasha Hetzel

ALMACEN & BOTILLERIA

Las Acacias

EXPENDIO DE BE_
BIDAS ALCOHOLICAS
GIRO MINIMERCADO
CLASE H-
VALOR

ERES MI
MEJOR AMIGO DEL
BARRIO

Escudo
MAS CERVEZA

$700

Escudo

Escudo

Escud

TOP Punta de Lobos opened the door to the possibilities of giant surf along the Chilean coastline. BOTTOM Santos del Mar was discovered and Ramón found out that he wasn't immortal. Photos: Alfredo Escobar

NEXT SPREAD This secret break, which Ramón pioneered, could be one of the best big-wave spots in the world. Photo: Daniel Russo

02   The Search
      for More

The Guide

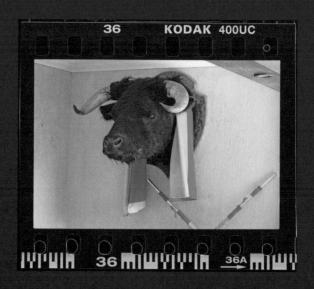

Photos by Patrick Trefz

Ramón's actions speak louder than any words could.
His vision for the Chilean coastline is not to hoard it or keep it to
himself; he wants to share it with like-minded people. He has helped
introduce Chile's waves to everyone from traveling backpackers to
the best surfers in the world. Photos: Patrick Trefz

APX 400

261

59

59

APX 100   436

47   A   AGFA   48   AGFA

You know there are just so many undiscovered waves, it's almost overwhelming. All of those big waves and not enough time and not enough resources to check them all and find the next Jaws—which is what we're all looking for really. He dragged me off to this slab, one year, Santos del Mar I think it was. We had to launch skis through a pounding shorebreak. The ski got rolled and almost crushed us while we were pushing it in. He took me out there to this mutant, barely-rideable slab on your forehand, and then they whipped me into a couple on my backhand. It was a terrifying experience to tell you the truth. — Grant Baker

NEXT SPREAD In 2007 the ASP came to Northern Chile to hold an event at a spot called El Gringo. On the first morning a giant swell hit and the contest directors decided it was too big and stormy to hold the event. While the best surfers in the world watched, Ramón paddled out by himself and packed the biggest closeouts. Photo: Alfredo Escobar

EXPLORA—TIONS

by Dusty Middleton

In Ramón's earliest years, before he had ever touched a surfboard or examined the waves, his father, Alejandro, taught him to freedive. Ramón learned about the sea in the frigid water, wielding homemade tools and wearing thick rubber suits. Alejandro taught his boy that the ocean in front of their home would provide a livelihood. It would put food on the table.

As a toddler, climbing along the rocks of Punta de Lobos, listening closely and learning from his father, young Ramón became a Chilean fisherman. Ramón, like Alejandro, would survive by the sea. He would live content and confident with his abilities.

In the Chilean culture of the fishermen, divers, and seaweed collectors, the art of their conversations and greetings, their rhymes, jokes, and limericks passed down through the generations are akin to a verbal test to know for certain whether you are one of them. Ramón's connection with the wit and language of this extended family is a key part of his personality and his identity.

———

A thousand miles to the north, as a focused young man with shiny sunglasses, a crisp baseball hat, and a Jeep piled high with surfboards, Ramón Navarro's polite greeting and conversations with weathered fishermen are a favorite part of any day. The knowledge these simple men have of their coastline, the currents, and offshore slabs is invaluable. Their jokes and rhymes always bring Ramón belly laughter and delight.

It's morning and we stop at a crude little lean-to shack and say hello to the lone *pescador* for this stretch of twenty miles of rock and sea. As I watch and listen to their conversation—much too fast for gringo ears—I observe the old fisherman light up with recognition as Ramón answers back in the proper rhymes and cadence. The old man nods along, grins, and knows right away that Ramón is part of his extended family.

They trade jokes and rhymes. Laugh. Stare out at the horizon. Discuss the sea and the wind, and wish each other a good day.

"This Viejo, he tells a classic one," Ramón chuckles as we get back in the Jeep, calling out, "*Adiós, nos vemos.*" Ramón waves and continues slowly on south.

Intelligent word play and humor, the sing-songy rhymes and riddles of these meetings go a long way. This is a harsh and lonely coastline where a once-a-week truck driver who sells water might be a fisherman's only human visitor for months on end.

———

LEFT On the road somewhere in the high desert of Northern Chile. Photo: Crystal Thornburg-Homcy BELOW There are hidden gems if you are willing to go off the beaten track. Photos: Rodrigo Farias Moreno

Ramón and I have been camping our way south from Chile's northern border, driving along washboard dirt roads that wind along low cliffs. A thin cloud of red dirt kicked up from our tires drops slowly behind us in the still air. The ocean has been smooth and clear, the mid-day sky, bright and cloudless.

The Atacama Desert is said to be the driest in the world. And though there's not an abundance of life up on land, the ocean is overflowing with it. We have eaten like kings: Mask, wetsuit, fins, and a reliable speargun keep our bellies full.

Ramón's curiosity to explore this stretch of Chile began years earlier. He had been a quiet teenager listening to his Walkman, his face pressed to the window of a passenger bus. Traveling north to Iquique to compete in a surf contest he had his first taste of the vastness, the emptiness, and the freedom of his country. On the rare occasions, during that thirty-hour bus ride, when the ocean came into view, he had been captivated.

The Panamericana, the proper north–south road, veers far from the ocean for large stretches of its thousand-mile journey, and it's on one of those stretches that we have been making our way, slowly in four-wheel drive, mapping and surfing. This is a wave-rich land; around every bend and cove the deep water and shallow reefs show their potential. Much of Ramón's adult life has been dedicated to searching his country's immense coast and learning its secrets.

The fishermen in this region tell Ramón that they have seen cars with surfboards only a few times in these last ten years. But they had never seen the waves in front of their camps ridden, until we paddled out.

———

We've spent a month camping along this coast and we're near the southern edge of the Atacama and the swell is pumping today. We park on a bluff overlooking a sharp bay and walk to the edge of a small cliff to study this wave and drink a maté.

The ocean is moving. Rip currents are sliding fast along the rocks. There is no sand or soft spot to exit the water for miles in either direction, just sharp rocks, *erizo* (sea urchin), and *picorocos* (tube corals). We wear booties here as much to keep our feet intact as to keep them warm.

Offshore there's a shifting, heavy A-frame. We guess that it's equal with full-size Sunset. The lip is throwing in slow motion, and the air is thick with salt. The inside right looks treacherous and too fast. The wave is complicated and untrustworthy.

After watching this peak for an hour we decide that today is not the day. Too much rip. Too much chaos. Like dozens of other world-class waves, Ramón will tuck this one away in his brain and return again in the future.

We drive a few miles farther south and come across a nice peak that likely has never been surfed before.

We spend twenty minutes watching while pulling boards from the racks and suiting up. We agree that this wave looks solid, and we're out there. It's funny that the safe choice is a ten-foot bowling left. Ramón air-drops down the face of his first wave, and snaps up into a thick, exitless barrel.

Our month of surf exploration is almost over, but the impressive quiet of this stretch of Northern Chile will have us back. The camping is so good. The spearfishing, so good. The days spent hunting great waves never before surfed, so enjoyable.

As we sit at the campfire that night, leaning against boulders, warming up a pot of *navegado* and thinking back to the different waves we have encountered, I ask about the old fisherman we met this morning. I'm curious about the *dicho*, the rhyme that the pescador shared that had made Ramón laugh.

Ramón nods, grinning, and pours out two cups of the warm vino.

"The Viejo tells us this one, I know it from a long time ago: '*Dejar que la niña pene, pene sus penas de amor, que para la pena que tiene mientras mas pene … mejor.*'"

Ramón repeats it slowly until I can wrap my brain around it. Each day these *dichos* have been my ongoing Spanish lessons. He translates the play on words and chuckles. We sit back and listen to the surf. Tomorrow the dirt track we are on meets the paved road and we will return to civilization.

We both agree, sitting there in the dirt next to our tents, that this life in the Atacama is a fine one, and that the ocean surely does provide.

Kohl Christensen.
Photo: Rodrigo Farias Moreno

TOP Central Chilean coastline. Photo: Alfredo Escobar BOTTOM 'Big Ben,' Kohl, and Ramón banter over who is better with a 1970s engine. Photo: Juan Luis de Heeckeren

NEXT SPREAD With over 2,500 miles of coastline, Ramón and Kohl are just scratching the surface. Photo: Juan Luis de Heeckeren

Ramón has helped to prove that Chile's surf has as much power
and size as anywhere on earth. Photo: Alfredo Escobar

ABOVE With all the technology in the world today, Chile is still a place where you get your information from local fishermen and your heat from an open fire. Top photo: Sebastian Mueller, Middle photo: Alfredo Escobar, Bottom photo: Dylan Lucas Gordon

RIGHT Photo: Jeff Johnson

Sea Change

Photos by Jeff Johnson, Alfredo Escobar,
Juan Luis de Heeckeren,
Scott Soens, Grant Ellis, & Todd Glaser

RAMÓN'S FIRST VISIT REMEM— BERED

by Kohl Christensen

I had met Ramón on my first trip to Chile in 1996. I came back to Hawai'i, saved some money, and flew back to Chile in '98. I hung out for quite a while. When I got back to O'ahu I decided to move up to the North Shore from Kailua. I kind of knew that Ramón might be coming; I was pretty much his only contact in Hawai'i.

Sure enough, Ramón showed up, but he didn't show up by himself. He showed up with Diego Medina, and he brought a boogie boarder named Vaca. None of them could speak any English. Really bad. Vaca couldn't speak a lick of it. Diego was worse, and Ramón was even worse. And between the three of them they had about a hundred bucks.

I didn't have any money at the time. I had just got back from traveling and I was between construction jobs. So I put them up in my house. And we figured out where all the free food was. There was a church in La'ie you had to take the bus to. Every Tuesday morning they gave away food. And there was the purple van that drove around and gave out food. And then there was another church in Hale'iwa that gave out groceries.

Ramón's a good baker and I helped them build a mud oven in the backyard. They started selling empanadas. Vaca stood on the side of the road trying to sell empanadas, but no one would stop. He just looked filthy: bare feet; covered in mud; with the empanadas in a shitty, red cooler. And he'd stand out there for hours. They never earned much.

One day they sold their whole load of empanadas to some construction workers ... but the whole crew got indigestion. My mom might have been their biggest client. She had a couple of dinner parties and placed some big orders.

Besides that, they were just surfing. They had no real care. They would steal my truck and steal my boards.

———

That winter we took Freed's fishing boat over to Maui, and we crashed into Lana'i and got marooned. We were stuck there until we fixed the propeller. We spearfished for menpachi, and Ramón proved to be quite the spearfisher. He had never used a three-prong before, but he was really good at it.

That was a wild trip. We got caught in some storms, and eventually made it to Maui and hung out there for a couple weeks.

We caught an eight-foot shark on the way back and Ramón made the decision to keep it, clean it, and store the meat in milk. It was good meat for the winter. We lived off that shark for months.

———

That was fifteen years ago: 1999. We were just kids. Who would have thought we'd be surfing in the Eddie Aikau together? I don't think it was a goal for either of us back then; we just liked surfing big waves. And ten years later, we're surfing together in the Eddie.

Ramón is one of the most successful athletes in Chile. He has multiple national and international sponsors. He makes a very good living for himself. He's not stealing from Foodland or digging through trashcans for food anymore.

And now we're on the same surf team, which is pretty neat. We ride the same boards. Ramón's boards are actually a little thicker than mine.

Ten years from now we'll still be surfing together. Family men. Still surfing strong. Chasing swells. I can't see either of us ever walking away from the sea. We both have been so connected with the sea throughout our lives in different ways. And it's brought us so much.

Photo: Juan Luis de Heeckeren

Ramón arrived in Hawai'i with no surfboards and one hundred dollars in his pocket. After a crash course on surfing big waves from Kohl, while surviving on homemade empanadas and wild chickens, Ramón returned to Chile. A decade of commitment later he was selected by his peers to surf in the Eddie Aikau, the most prestigious big-wave event in the world. Photos: Jeff Johnson

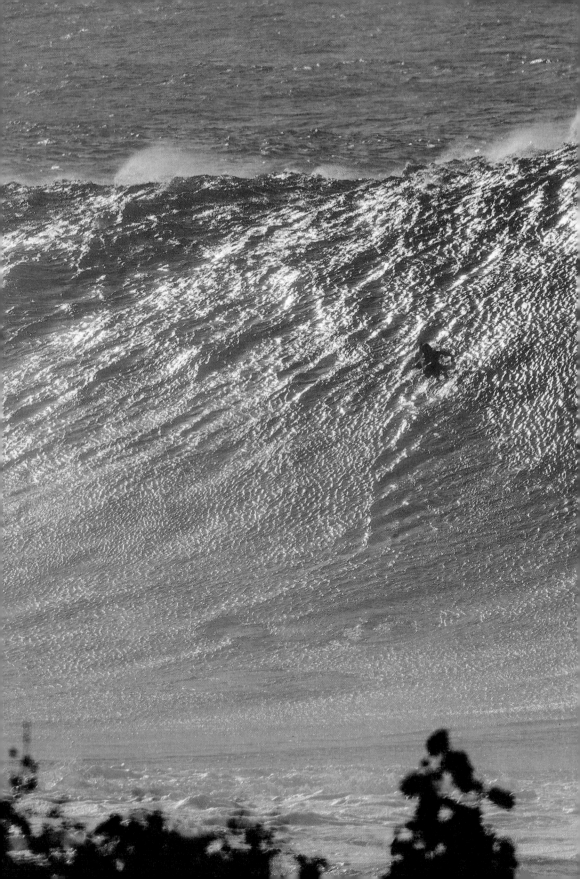

I was so stoked to see Ramón in the [Eddie] contest. He easily deserved to be in that event … because when a wave comes, he's going to go. He'll just spin around and take off. His heat was the heat of the event, so many big waves came in that one hour. When Ramón's came I remember the whole crowd was just like "Whaaaaaa!" You could see that wave like a mile out, and he was only on like a 9'2" or a 9'4", he wasn't on one of the biggest boards.

I remember when he caught it going "Oh my God, that's Ramón. Sick!" It's just such a good feeling when you see a guy who's not a super-well-known guy in the surf world at that point, and all of a sudden within five seconds everyone knew who Ramón was. He got to the bottom and it blasted all around him and he came out and the whole crowd just went crazy.

I got goose-bumps all up my back. It was crazy to watch that in person. You knew that guy's life was changing in some way right then, significantly. — Kelly Slater

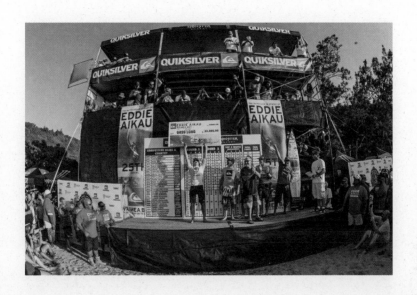

The Eddie Aikau was held December 8, 2009, at Waimea Bay in
giant surf. The surf pulsed in the afternoon to a size that hadn't
been seen in years. Ramón caught, and was rewarded for, the
biggest wave of the event, and was transformed. He ran up the
beach into the arms of his pregnant wife, Paloma, and into
surfing's history. Photos: Grant Ellis

At Waimea the waves that break at twenty-five feet break in the exact same spot as they do when it is eighteen feet. You can see these gargantuan sets coming for ages—everyone's screaming on the hill and on the rocks, and everyone's getting nervous in the lineup, and a lot of people start paddling out to sea to get over the waves. But if you want to catch one of those waves you have to just sit there and hold your position, because as soon as you get off that ledge, you won't catch a wave, no matter how big your board is, no matter how bad you want it. It's a weird mind game where you have to turn everything off and just say to yourself, "Okay, I'm not moving."

It was pretty impressive to see Ramón not moving, not paddling too far out. He just put his head down and totally committed. He knifed into the wave right on the apex and being backside it was just radical. You need a lot of ability to be able to do that. I think it was such a game changer for him personally. I think it's probably going to stand out when he looks back on his life. — Shane Dorian

Greg Long, Ramón Navarro, and Ian Walsh celebrate the spirit of Eddie Aikau. Photo: Todd Glaser

03 Protecting His Own

The Impact Zone

Photos by Jeff Johnson

OF HEARTS AND HANDS

by Josh Berry

Pichilemu, Ramón Navarro's hometown and the country's burgeoning surf capital, was deeply agitated because of a government proposal to build a sewage pipeline at La Puntilla, the town's central surf spot. The pipeline and the town's poorly maintained beaches threatened surfers, tourism, and everything good that this town knew.

With an organization named Proplaya—a group of surfers dedicated to environmental action for Chile's mistreated coastline—Ramón and I planned a volunteer cleanup at the municipal beach in Pichilemu. Then plans went slightly south.

The town's mayor at the time thought our volunteer event was a bad idea—he supported the construction of the sewage pipeline, and didn't want anyone to believe that his beach needed cleaning by a ragtag crew of volunteer citizens. The day before our scheduled beach cleanup, the mayor sent a crew of municipal workers to pick up all the trash on the beach. He wanted to prove us wrong and claim credit for a trash-free beach.

Ramón and the crew of locals gathered that morning were pissed off, because we knew that the mayor had sent his workers to pick up trash. News travels fast in rural Chile and there are no secrets here. All assembled were upset, but we still had a job to do. There was plenty of garbage to find in the dunes if we walked just a little farther.

About twenty of us were shivering in the early morning fog, distributing trash bags and offering words of encouragement. Ramón stepped forward and in a loud voice said, "When we're done here, let's take all this trash back to our mayor! He knows what to do with it." We laughed and then we were on our way.

An hour later I'd collected two large bags full of trash from the dunes and beach grass. Most of it was wind-blown plastic from tourists visiting the beach, or weathered plastic washed ashore from sea. Lugging all this back to the parking lot where we had started, it was inspiring to see others doing the same thing. I added my pickings to the growing pile of black garbage bags.

Ramón was there again speaking passionately: "Seriously, let's take this garbage to the town hall. The mayor finally cleaned our beach for us yesterday; he should know what to do with all this crap, too! If he thinks he can solve our problems like this, we can bring our garbage to his door."

I followed the caravan behind Ramón's truck full of garbage and we made the trek through the dusty streets of Pichilemu. We unloaded our heavy bags of garbage into a neat pile on the steps of town hall and hung some bags from the building's wrought-iron gates. Someone left a polite note: "Mr. Mayor, please dispose of properly." We had cleaned our beach. We had made our feelings known as surfer-citizens. The story made the local news and our efforts were applauded.

Soon after, the mayor was removed from public office for receiving bribes. Then the sewage pipeline was defeated after a long and difficult battle—thanks in no small part to Ramón's efforts against corrupt small-town politicians and his loud voice calling attention to the value of their world-class local surf breaks.

LEFT Picking up trash is just one part of Ramón's plan to preserve Punta de Lobos for future generations. Photos: Rodrigo Farias Moreno BELOW Top photo: Sebastian Mueller, Bottom photo: Dylan Lucas Gordon

THIS SPREAD Ramón will be the first to remind you
that he is only the voice of a growing number of
stewards along the Chilean coastline. Photos:
Rodrigo Farías Moreno

e place of his

A SHAKEN COM— MUNITY

by Will Carless

Buildings swayed like reeds, then collapsed. Roads tore open like zippers, devouring cars and trees. Then, after the shaking, walls of water smashed into Chile's coastline, sucking everything in their path back out into the dark Pacific.

During the early morning hours of February 27, 2010, Chile was hit with one of the most powerful earthquakes in modern history. The magnitude 8.8 quake combined with a series of tsunamis ripped across Central Chile. News of the devastation went global instantly along with tsunami warnings for the entire Pacific Rim.

Ramón Navarro didn't feel a thing.

At 3:34 a.m. when the earthquake hit, Navarro was nestled in a LAN Airlines seat, somewhere high above the Pacific Ocean, bound for California. Oblivious to the devastation playing out below, he whizzed at hundreds of miles an hour away from his country and family.

It was only when he landed in Los Angeles that he discovered the disaster unfolding at home. The news was plastered across TV screens at LAX, but with phones and internet down (or swamped), he and his fellow passengers couldn't contact friends or family.

Frantic, Navarro ran to the airline counter and pleaded to buy a ticket back to Santiago. First and foremost in his mind was his wife, Paloma, eight and a half months pregnant with their first son and under strict orders to take it easy.

"She had just been to the doctor, and he had told her that she must completely avoid any stress!" Navarro said. "I was just freaking out."

But he couldn't get home. The airport in Santiago, where Navarro had boarded the plane the night before, had sustained major damage. No flights would be going in or out. Navarro was stuck.

Fellow big-wave surfers Greg Long and Kohl Christensen were at LAX to pick up their amigo Ramón. They'd heard the morning news. They knew things were bad, but they were damned if they were going to let their Chilean brother sit at the airport wringing his hands.

So, they convinced Navarro to get in Long's van, and drove south, stopping only at a café to mine the internet for more information about the disaster: How was his wife, Paloma? Did their house hold up? Were any of his friends or family hurt? Or worse? Ramon was desperate to hear his people were safe.

His nerves frayed, Navarro finally connected with his family. He learned they were thoroughly shaken and dealing with frequent aftershocks but fine. They told him the quake lasted forever and at least three tsunamis hit the coast. But news outside of town was hard to come by; the extent of damage and fate of some of his closest friends was still unknown.

With no way to get home for at least a few days, Navarro decided to do what he had come to do: surf giant waves—this time at a rarely held competition at Todos Santos Island, off Mexico's Northern Baja coast. And Todos was huge.

Despite his preoccupations, Ramon charged to the final, where he placed third behind Shane Dorian and Mark Healey. In between heats, lurching panga rides, and hold downs Navarro absorbed any news he could get from Chile; with the 8.8 quake, tsunamis, and 7+ magnitude aftershocks it was clear Chile's Central Coast—Ramon's coast—was hit hard. The coast that had raised him needed his help.

That weekend, just hours after the quake, Long, Christensen, and fellow California charger Noel Robinson (who passed away tragically just a few months later surfing in Mexico) had made up their minds: They were

BELOW Photo: Rodrigo Farias Moreno

going to Chile to help Ramon. Save the Waves, who had been working on environmental threats to Chile's coast with Navarro, dropped everything and committed to run the campaign. Patagonia offered support and Waves for Water would help source water filters.

On the ground, Ramon's friend and colleague Quinn Campbell bought food, blankets, and water to hand out within striking distance of Chris Wilcox's language school, which was the effort's improvised Pichilemu headquarters. Ramon's dad (Jano), Cristian Merello, Diego Medina, Gavin Comstock, Phillip Muller, Pancho Veliz, Rodrigo Farias, and other Chilean surfers signed up to help. Word spread fast.

In San Clemente, supplies piled up in Long's garage: duffels full of clothing, tents for shelter, medical essentials, and water filters.

As the "Fuerza Chile" relief effort grew, Navarro was on the first plane back to Chile where he rejoined his family. Quinn remembers Ramon jumping off the plane and heading straight to the radio station to broadcast, "If you can help, and haven't yet, you'll come lend a hand tomorrow." And they did.

A few days later, Long, Christensen, and Robinson boarded a plane for Chile, loaded with mountains of relief supplies. "Miraculously, the airlines let them check something like twenty-four giant bags once they knew what they were doing," Navarro said. Other supplies were en route via air shipments.

The Fuerza Chile effort expanded in reach and size. Navarro's team covered Pichilemu to Constitución, while farther south, Save the Waves' Josh Berry worked with Coastkeeper's Rodrigo de la O, local surfers, and the late Paul Walker and his REACT doctors. In the US, support poured from the surf community and beyond: Rob Machado, Kelly Slater, Jackson Browne, Dawes, Jack Johnson, Andrew Bird, Thomas Campbell, Shepard Fairy, Jon Swift, Wolfgang Bloch, Robert Trujillo, Kirk Hammett, Brushfire Records, the extended Malloy family, and countless others rallied behind the cause.

The volunteers on the ground delivered tents, tarps, clothing, food, blankets, water filters, and immeasurable amounts of goodwill.

They visited rural coastal towns that were ravaged. They found communities battered but united and thankful to know that people cared. Chile's biggest television channels reported, seemingly to their surprise, how bands of surfers showed up to bring relief to the coastal communities most in need.

In some cases they would help old friends and fellow surfers, like Constitución mainstay Pocha, whose house had washed away. Pocha, who had hosted so many surfers in Constitución, lost nearly everything.

Weeks into the campaign, aftershocks still growled and rumbled under foot. The volunteers slept on high ground until threats of tsunamis eased.

THIS PAGE Top photo: Geoff Ragatz, Bottom photos: Philip Muller

Maybe their volunteerism was emblematic of the bond formed while facing life-threatening situations together in the water. But the mission to Chile was instinctive. "Navarro didn't plead with anyone," Long said. "We just knew that going was the right thing to do."

According to Long, "Ramon has always stood out in the surfing community. He's an ambassador for surfers, but he's also just an ambassador for humanity itself."

For his part, the relief effort was giving back to the ocean and communities that have shaped his very being. "It was a way of showing respect," he said, "I know who's the boss ... the main boss in my life is the ocean." Navarro said he was humbled and incredibly grateful for the outpouring of support for his community when it was really needed. He was also profoundly inspired by seeing the good that can be achieved when enough people get behind the right cause.

THIS SPREAD Rapa Nui is a tiny island far removed from civilization. Every time Ramón goes there he brings boards and gear for the local kids. Photos: Rodrigo Farias Moreno NEXT SPREAD For Ramón the ocean is a spiritual place; he always takes time to give thanks. Photo: Rodrigo Farias Moreno

Fire & Ice

Photos by Rodrigo Farias Moreno,
Alfredo Escobar, & Juan Luis de Heeckeren

The first time I met Ramón was surfing out at Himalayas, which [at the time] was our own private twenty-foot pipeline. Kohl brought him out there, and basically anybody who can punch through all those lineups just to get out to that outside reef deserves to be out there—Ramón was out there, and he was charging. — Dave Wassel

04 Taking the Stage

FOR THE LOVE OF SURF— ING

by Gerry Lopez

Ramón Navarro is an outstanding surfer but only in the last ten years have we heard his name. This level of expertise isn't just gained in a decade, so how is it possible that one of the truly great big-wave surfers of our generation is only now becoming known?

To develop good surfing skills—given the prerequisite desire, determination, athleticism, aptitude, and an innate connection with the ocean—one needs lots of surf. But only with a particular mind-set can one rise above the field.

Fear plays a big part in the development of all surfers—fear of failure, fear of the sea, of sharks, of anything the mind can conjure to be afraid of. It is in the process of learning to cope and overcome these fears that some surfers set themselves apart from all the rest. In finding an affinity for big surf, there is another level of fear to deal with: the very real fear that the power of the waves can easily overcome the strongest, bravest, most stalwart of surfers and hold them under the water until their air runs out. And maybe the big waves magnify that fear of the unknowable, unthinkable, or unimaginable. The physical side of surfing is difficult enough by itself to master, but it is the mental part that makes or breaks the endeavor.

In the United States, Australia, or any of the major surfing countries, the surfers who prevail through these struggles best are closely watched and coached, often emerging as fully formed surf stars while still teenagers. In a country like Chile, with consistent and excellent surf, a surfer like Ramón, with superbly developed skills, can and has appeared on the surf scene like a comet, wonderfully shocking the surf world. Of course, because of Ramón, Chile is now a known entity and any more comets like him will be heralded before they show up. Ramón has arrived and his craft, like his notoriety, continues to rise.

During the 2012 Volcom Fiji Pro, a big swell was in the forecast and many, if not most, of the big-wave specialists were there when it came. This ASP World Tour event is a big deal with the top thirty-two professional surfers and all the gear and people that accompany a contest of this size, definitely maxing out the capacity of Tavarua and Namotu islands. Add all the big-wave guys and their big-wave boards and it is an extravaganza of significant proportions.

Perhaps it was destiny, but for reasons unknown the contest was put on hold as the swell began to peak. This allowed anyone who wanted into the water for what would become one of the best big-wave, free-surfing sessions in history. Cloudbreak was at its all-time best with many waves in the fifteen- to twenty-foot range and some even bigger.

Cloudbreak is a unique setup with a deep-water channel and a prevailing trade wind that blows offshore ... more or less. The ending of the wave is nebulous as it runs into the aptly named Shish Kabob reef, where a closeout or even a cleanly executed exit into a wide-swinging set results in some absolutely terrifying moments. You don't want to be caught inside on this very shallow section of very sharp coral.

The offshore winds are often in the nuclear range, hanging a surfer in the lip of an already steep takeoff. The storms generated in the Roaring Forties push powerful swells between Australia and New Zealand—and directly at this reef pass in Fiji. There isn't anything playful about Cloudbreak. At three to five feet, it is a fast, hollow wave that packs a wallop. In the six- to eight-foot range, it is world class and dangerous. When it gets to ten to twelve feet, it is in a whole other realm as the swell swings down the reef, doubling up into a classic ledge takeoff that is for experts only and often leaving them baffled or hoping for mercy on a failed attempt. Getting caught inside at Cloudbreak when it's big is not an experience for the faint

Ramón's first session in Fiji during the 2012 historic swell at Tavarua Island. Photo: Fred Pompermayer

of heart; it is as scary and perilous as it gets. Cloudbreak at fifteen to twenty feet is another solar system.

Dawn patrol on Thursday saw the swell had arrived and was still rising. When the contest was put on hold, the lineup that filled the water was impressive, including Ramón, Mark Healey, Ian Walsh, Nathan Fletcher, Grant Baker, Kohl Christensen, Reef McIntosh, Jamie Sterling, Jamie Mitchell, Alex Gray, Dave Wassel, Danny Fuller, and many of the ASP surfers, none with big enough surfboards for the conditions. The waves were off the scale.

The surfing was equally incredible even though some waves did come through where the surfers just got out of the way and let them by. One wave of particularly gargantuan size caught Mark Healey out of position, causing him to peel off his leash and swim for his life. The image of his ten-foot gun looking tiny on the heaving, impossibly thick lip of a massive tube that would have stretched the limits of a thirty-foot tape measure is just one of the many timeless pictures from that session. Reef McIntosh and Ian Walsh got memorable waves, big beautiful tubes without a drop of water out of place.

It was Ramón's wave that really stood out for me. It wasn't one of biggest, but it was not small by any means. If one were measuring, the wave would have been fifteen feet tall where Ramón dropped in. At Cloudbreak at this size, there is no easy entry; Ramón used all ten feet of his board to scratch his way into this beast.

What thoughts were going through his mind as he got to his feet to begin his journey down this wave? He could see it stretched out far ahead, the other surfers looking down from the shoulder or paddling hard to get out of the way, and only one way to get to the other end, all of it super critical. Yet at this moment, he was poised, focused, and relaxed. It seemed as if the wave lurched up bigger as Ramón laid into his turn under the heaving lip. Again he needed every inch of his gun to hug the steep wall and hold a line on the thick tube as it sucked water up the face trying to take him and his board with it.

Then he was there, deep within the bowels of this meaty monster, racing it as it tried to eat him. The foam ball built behind him, threatening to roll him up. At one point it came underneath his board and bucked him violently but he managed to hang on and slip away from it. Mick Fanning, one of the very best surfers in the entire world, screamed his excitement of witnessing the ride from a ringside seat on the shoulder as Ramón slid by, still deep in the tube.

It was a stunning ride—an entry into the XXL Big Wave Ride of the Year—but maybe just another wave in the life of Ramón Navarro, who does it for the best of reasons ... because he loves it. Keep surfing.

Photos: Fred Pompermayer

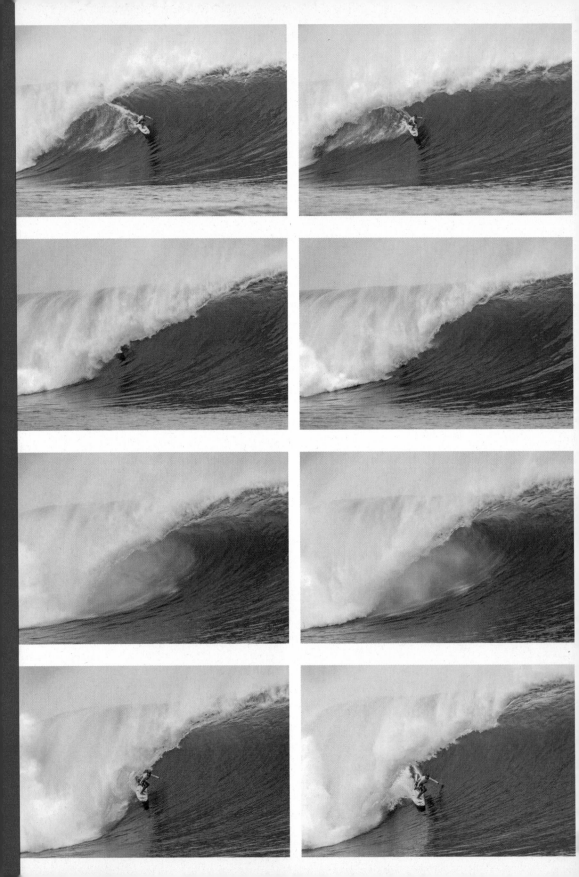

We were in Fiji for that swell. All the best big-wave surfers were there. I saw Ramón on one and at first I was thinking, "Oh no, he's too deep. He's going to just get flogged!" But he had just taken off and driven into it. And he was gone. Then he went over a foam ball. Then another section fell and he did exactly the same thing. His board just floating like he was on a six-footer or something. My heart was in my mouth for him because I thought he was dead, and he just kept floating over these foam balls ... it was the craziest thing I've ever seen. – Mick Fanning

PREVIOUS SPREAD Photos: Tom Servais RIGHT A grateful Ramón. Photo: Fred Pompermayer

A WORLD SURF— ING RESERVE

by Nick Mucha

What do you do if private investors want to build large-scale commercial projects along the rugged coastline that you call home? If you are Ramón Navarro wanting to protect Punta de Lobos, Chile, you team up with Save The Waves, get the site approved as a World Surfing Reserve, and together you mount a focused campaign to undermine the developers' audacious plans.

In response to these looming threats, a passionate group of local surfers, environmentalists, government officials, and business leaders in Pichilemu, Chile—where Punta de Lobos is located—banded together behind the leadership of their local surf hero. They committed themselves to take control of the situation and build legal protection for Lobos' iconic left-hand break, rich marine environment, and the subsistence fishing heritage. Their first action was to submit a World Surfing Reserve application to Save The Waves Coalition in September 2013.

Save The Waves Coalition, a California-based nonprofit organization committed to preserving and protecting the coastal environment, oversees the prestigious World Surfing Reserve (WSR) program. They receive dozens of applications a year from coastal communities around the world that seek to secure protection for their local surf breaks. The WSR program is highly selective and only a few choice breaks around the world have qualified for the designation. Six to be exact: Malibu, California; Manly Beach, Australia; Ericeira, Portugal; Santa Cruz, California; Huanchaco, Peru; and Bahía de Todos Santos, Baja California.

The program proactively identifies, designates, and preserves outstanding waves, surf zones, and their surrounding environments. The program serves as a global model for preserving wave breaks and their surrounding areas by recognizing the positive environmental, cultural, economic, and community benefits of surfing areas. This global network of Surfing Reserves is designed to educate the world about the tremendous value of these special places and provides the planning and tools necessary to help local communities better protect their cherished breaks.

An international panel of respected surfers, scientists, and environmentalists, known as the Vision Council, routinely evaluates new WSR applications. The Vision Council reviews each application against four criteria: (1) quality and consistency of the wave, (2) environmental characteristics of the area, (3) surf culture and history of the area, and (4) local community support.

Despite the highly selective nature of this program it is no surprise that Punta de Lobos was approved to become the next World Surfing Reserve. The point is renowned for its world-class surf, vibrant local culture, robust marine ecosystem, and beautiful topography. The famous left-hand pointbreak works from three to thirty feet, and is frequented by the world's elite big-wave surfers. Chile's surfing history can be traced here, with Lobos being one of the first waves to be surfed consistently by visiting and local surfers alike.

Punta de Lobos not only provides a playground for surfers, but is also one of the most unique coastal landscapes in Chile, with the iconic Morros and beautiful headlands gracing the point. Punta de Lobos supports a rich coastal and marine ecosystem, including plentiful fish, crustaceans, endemic cactus and bird species, and is a migratory stopping point for gray whales.

Ramón Navarro was born and raised in the magnificence of the area and was the first to rally the other concerned local coastal advocates together to protect it. His leadership and vision for Punta de Lobos is, no doubt, the catalyst for it being a World Surfing Reserve today.

Currently, the entire point is under private ownership. The current zoning regulations allow for new construction and at least one large-scale

PREVIOUS SPREAD Although Punta de Lobos offers some of the best big lefts in the world, it is also one of the most consistent and playful waves in South America. Photo: Rodrigo Farias Moreno

LEFT Photo: Rodrigo Farias Moreno
BELOW Ramón's biggest hero, his mother, Maria. Photo: Jeff Johnson

condominium project has been proposed. If unchecked, Punta de Lobos could be transformed beyond recognition and the multigenerational subsistence fishermen would be replaced by private access developments and construction crews.

Save The Waves and the local WSR committee have been effective so far in holding back the tide of unchecked development along the fabled point. The long-term vision is to protect the coastline of Punta de Lobos and make it a permanent public space for all to enjoy. Especially those who love long, powerful lefts in a remarkable setting.

BELOW Punta de Lobos is where a rich ocean meets an equally rich land; the point's history is one of fishing and ranching. Photo: Jeff Johnson RIGHT Photo: Rodrigo Farias Moreno FOLLOWING SPREAD Photo: Juan Luis de Heeckeren

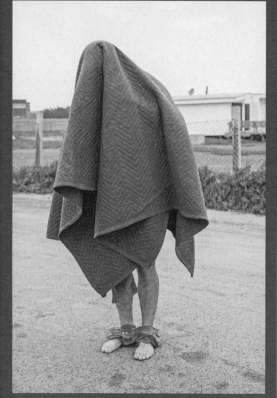